THE CAI AUTHOR/INSTRUCTOR

THE CAI AUTHOR/INSTRUCTOR

An introduction and guide to the independent preparation of computer-administerable instructional materials in the conversational mode.

J.C. Meredith

Indiana University, Bloomington, Indiana

Educational Technology Publications
Englewood Cliffs, New Jersey 07632

Printed in the United States of America.

Library of Congress Catalog Card Number: 70-125876.

International Standard Book Number: 0-87778-014-5.

First Printing

ACKNOWLEDGEMENTS

This *Introduction and Guide* was prepared during the time the author served as program manager of an Office of Education project of the Institute of Library Research, University of California (Berkeley), entitled "An Information Processing Laboratory for Education and Research in Library Science" (OEG-1-7-71085-4286). The observations and recommendations set forth herein, although not within the purview of that project, were derived in part from the associated experience of implementing several units of computer-assisted instruction in aspects of librarianship, as one component of the model laboratory.

The encouragement of Professor M.E. Maron, School of Librarianship and associate director of the Institute of Library Research, led to this separate undertaking, and the author is most grateful to him and to Mr. Ralph M. Shoffner, project coordinator of the Institute, for their detailed criticisms and suggestions.

CONTENTS

THE CAI AUTHOR/INSTRUCTOR

INTRODUCTION

1.

INTRODUCTION

It has been said that "CAI is a phenomenon in search of a theory of instruction (Silvern, 1966)." Since 1966, the number of individuals and organizations actively engaged in both the theoretical and the technical aspects of computer-assisted instruction have increased manyfold. The bare task of keeping track of the current literature in the field has become a problem in itself, to say nothing of the deeper perplexities of evaluating different approaches and of identifying the most promising for use in a given situation.

That the technology is developing very rapidly in spite of formidable obstacles should surprise no one who is aware of CAI's potential impact upon education. However, this development has been very uneven, especially in respect to the central function of *authorship.*

This function was outlined in the 1966 paper quoted above, by Gloria M. and Leonard C. Silvern, entitled "Computer-assisted instruction: specifications for CAI programs and programmers." They spoke of the "instructional programmer" as a person who (1) performs job and task analysis, (2) establishes behavioral objectives, (3) devises criterion tests, (4) develops course outlines to the teaching point level, and (5) writes steps in the lesson plan. The authors went on to admit that, "Of all the specialists essential for the development and production of CAI, only the instructional programmer is a phantom . . . a figment of the imagination . . . " and that "The instructional programmer's skills are difficult to identify and even more difficult to impart."

Today these difficulties of identification and description still exist. The instructional programmer, although no longer a phantom, is fairly elusive.

For one thing, he is usually someone's alter ego, and an undernourished one at that. By this I mean that there has been a tendency on the part of those who design, program, install and operate a CAI system to be so preoccupied with the system itself that the actual preparation of corpus is slighted or put off to the last moment. One of them may whip up something in his own specialty, or perhaps Miss Jones down the hall will be asked to write up a string of lessons—"You know: make a statement, then ask a question about it, then have something to say about the student's answer, then make another statement and so on. Don't worry about not knowing how to do computer programming; we're using GABBLE, the new user-oriented CAI language."

Miss Jones may agree, unfortunately, without realizing the hidden demands of the task.

After working and re-working instructional corpus for a graduate course in librarianship, in the Institute for Library Research, University of California, we evolved what appears to be a viable methodology for the design, writing, encoding, testing, revision and validation of computer-assisted instruction (Maron *et al.,* 1969, Section III.) That portion of the methodology which underlies the writing, and those aspects of design and coding inseparable from the writing, form the basis for the recommendations set forth in this Guide. An effort will be made to separate this work from the other activities involved in creating an operational CAI installation, so that it can be carried out in advance of completed system design.

TEACHER-AS-AUTHOR

I propose to nominate an individual, a teacher, to carry out the function of course authorship. I will call him or her the *author/instructor,* or simply *author*—rather than "instructional programmer," which implies rather more coding responsibility than is appropriate. To clarify: even though there exist "high-level, user-oriented" CAI languages with which a novice can learn to work very readily, such initial facility is quite superficial. Nothing in CAI is as easy as it looks. The amount of mechanistic scheming and arranging needed to exploit a good CAI language, the placement of symbols and delimiters, the detection and analysis of errors—all take a good deal of time and attention. There are hidden constraints in every language, and the creators of computer languages are not very good at explaining them to amateurs. Trial and error tend to become standard procedure. An author/instructor who takes on the added responsibility for encoding his own output runs the risk of serious distraction.

I further propose that the teacher should take the initiative in finding out about CAI, and should think about what it could mean to his students and to his own corner of the profession. Do his favorite ideas on his specialty begin to lose their bloom, expressed over and over as they must be to a succession of classes? Can he fashion them into something definitive—his best—and let the machine take care of their replication? Can he divine enough of the learning process to shape and refine all manner of conversational gambits leading to its fulfillment?

The teacher who is to embark on CAI authorship should do so in the conviction that the new medium is worth exploring and in the knowledge, too, that answers will not be won easily. The decision to proceed should come from within; it should not be thrust upon him.

This is why I propose, lastly, that the author/instructor set to work as soon as he is ready to try his hand, *without* waiting for the reality (and the pressure) of a CAI installation-in-being at his own particular institution. In simplistic terms, it is a question of stature: who or what should determine the shape of CAI? Should it be a row of blind terminals saying, "Here we are; put us to work!" Or should it be the teacher, saying, "This is what I want to do in a CAI system"?

The author/instructor needs a running headstart to develop the requirements for the particular system he would like to have at his disposal. The best configuration for one kind and level of instruction may not do at all for another kind and level, but if the teacher is not in a position to assert a preference well ahead of time, the engineering, programming and cost considerations will eclipse all else.

There is a risk involved in taking the initiative: the risk of wasted effort. Suppose we examine this briefly.

Taking the worst case first, what if the CAI course put together so diligently never gets used? What if CAI itself never takes wing at Minimax College—doesn't even get hatched? Has the work of so many hours been wasted?

I think not. There are strong indications that the exercise of examining one's specialty anew in order to put it into machine-explainable form strengthens and freshens one's own concepts. When every idea to be put across must be justified and elucidated from a number of angles, the feebler ones are revealed not only to the teacher-as-author but to the teacher-as-lecturer as well. Writing an ordinary textbook doubtless increases one's subject competence; writing text that talks back toughens it. The script may wind up on the shelf, but not the analytical thinking which created it. That remains with the author.

What if the dialogue, as written, doesn't fit any particular CAI system?

Conversational CAI languages tend to converge into standard patterns of display statements and controls based on scansion of student input. If the author works in the vicinity of this convergence, he will find that his product—although it may not *look* like a computer program—will be compatible with one of these languages and as such will be readily encodable and executable.

A general risk, one which is incurred whether authorship is undertaken early or late, stems from the sheer magnitude of the task. No standard to indicate the number of man-hours required to generate one hour of student instruction exists—it all depends on the type of instruction, the student set, the relative freedom or rigidity of the system and last but not least the quality of the instruction. A ratio of 80:1 is sometimes offered as typical, but any ratio may be regarded as unique to a particular set of parameters which may never be duplicated.

The risk here (quite aside from the cost) lies in the fact that the magnitude of the investment can act as a deterrent to subsequent growth and change. Even minor revisions take a lot of trouble to implement. It is only human to postpone making them, or to settle for surface effect without regard to underlying pedagogical faults.

Somewhat related to this, and equally human, is a characteristic urge to defend our children. Having spent many hours in creating an instructional sequence, it hurts to have it blasted by others who have little understanding of the problems involved. For this there is no palliative. Such criticism is often not bestowed until everything is written, encoded and compiled in the computer—in short, is in the phase of operational testing. At this juncture, making changes is something like tearing a birthday cake apart after all the candles are lit, in order to change the flavor of the filling. Still, the author/instructor must be prepared to make changes in response to group opinion, with the best show of cheerfulness he can muster.

I don't think anyone who has read this far will be dissuaded by being told now that authorship of a CAI course is not a feat which is likely to win immediate recognition from one's co-professionals.

Recognition should become more tangible, however, as the calibre of CAI improves and as it becomes more generalizable. A definite change should occur as CAI becomes progressively more useful rather than merely interesting.

Much private pleasure and satisfaction can be gained from the writing of CAI. The teacher's confidence in the new medium will grow. He can surround himself with all kinds of imagined students and deal with each according to his desserts. He will be able to let himself go, rambling on as he likes, stopping here to polish a concept, stopping there to toss off an epigram.

Does he delight in elegant contrivances? An ingenious CAI frame is almost like a fine watch. Does he cherish individuality? There are literally millions of different paths through a sizeable CAI course. Does he look to the future? He will know that he is teaching in a way which may reshape his profession, in a way which is really new in the time of man.

"DIRECTED DIALOGUE"

Let us characterize the CAI author/instructor in such a way as to give more prominence to the writing function than can be inferred from the Silverns' description of the "instructional programmer." Let us say that he is one who, in pursuit of stated educational objectives, creates instructional text together with the specifications for the transfer of that text into a student-computer interactive system. He is the one who speaks to the student through the computer and it is to him that the student replies.

This Guide deals only with computer-assisted instruction of the kind often referred to as "conversational" or more accurately as "directed dialogue."

In this kind of CAI, words are the principal tools. We shall see how the computer deals with words by comparing them and how it uses these comparisons as bases for preplanned decisions. Beyond that, the inner workings of the computer need not concern us directly.

Directed dialogue CAI differs rather sharply from computational CAI, which deals mainly with mathematical and engineering concepts, usually in a drill-and-practice or problem-solving vein. In computational CAI, the student operates in a calculating-machine context, and the use of plain language on his part is rigorously limited. Such CAI programs are remarkably dynamic. They can supply data on demand, can analyze formulae, can assess unique student computations and can even generate new problems as they go along. Computer-assisted instruction of this type is usually engineered from the ground up for a particular installation.

To date, the intricacies of meaning within the English language have thwarted the efforts of computational linguists to bring a comparable degree of automation to conversational CAI. We must still prescribe in advance all meaningful discourse above the very simplest levels. And here we find that the peculiarities of the language, instead of hindering, can be very helpful indeed.

The recommendations in this manual are based on experience in the development of CAI dealing with fairly abstract concepts, in a mode which affords the student considerable latitude in expressing himself. Our work was aimed at graduate students of library science, but this kind of freedom should be useful at any level and may in the last analysis determine CAI's applicability to a large segment of the total curriculum.

A list of recommended readings for the prospective author/instructor is set forth in the Appendix. The list does not purport to cover the entire field, but only to serve as a frame of reference in which to consider CAI authorship as a new methodology within the teaching profession. Chapters 2, 3 and 4 of this Guide deal mainly with corpus, i.e., instructional substance, organization and expression. Chapters 5 and 6 introduce the reader to recommended methods of frame design. Chapter 7 discusses question design. Chapter 8 analyzes answer-types as an approach to scan specification. Chapters 9 and 10 illustrate methods of scan specification, branching, quoting, control, scoring and special subroutines.

CORPUS

2.

CORPUS

Before setting up a proposed course of instruction, the author needs to specify a number of parameters, which together will define the nature of his goal. He does this for his own guidance through the strange country ahead and will often need to review this definition in order to avoid losing his way.

A checklist of things to be specified begins with as accurate a description of corpus as can be devised: not simply to say what is to be included but also with special attention to that related material which shall be excluded and the proposed manner of its exclusion.

While distantly related material can be excluded tacitly, a formal statement governing adjacent material must be ready at hand. What kind of interface will be needed? Will the instruction always veer away from these interfaces or will it tolerate brief excursions into closely related topics? In any event the author should be prepared to apprise the student of the existence of these boundaries, whether solid or diffuse, so that the latter may perceive both the shape of the chosen corpus and its position in context.

If the material to be conveyed through CAI is envisaged as either supplementing or being supplemented by material conveyed in some other medium (lecture, reading, etc.) together forming an organic whole, their mutual interface does not need to be as clearly defined, provided the presentation is more or less concurrent. Where the other medium is rigid—as with prescribed reading—the burden is on the CAI portion to adapt, otherwise lacunae will be left unfilled. A more comfortable relationship exists between CAI and lecture modes; the latter can be counted on to reinforce the thin parts of the former, besides being well suited for presentation of background material, current developments and immediate applications, and to argue the fine distinctions which would be prohibitively intricate for CAI. If, on the other hand, supplementary material cannot be synchronized with the CAI portion, the latter must not only stand independently but may even be expected to provide some overlap.

The next item on the checklist is a definition of course objective(s), i.e., the conditions to be brought about in the student. What do you want him to know at the end which he may not have known at the beginning? With what new or improved skill is he to be endowed? If a clear statement in terms of task, objective and mission cannot be constructed, something is amiss.

At this point it will be necessary to characterize *student* rather closely. Consider first the median: how old is he? What are his resources in terms of background, general training and subject preparation? What are his typical aims? How widely are individuals in the student "set" distributed across medians? Even in a fairly homogeneous group it is likely that some members will deviate to such an extent that it will be uneconomical and perhaps even impossible to provide for them in the course you have in mind. The farther from the median along separate continua representing each of the above factors, the more laborious becomes the task of incorporating in a CAI course the requisite compensatory measures. A cut-off point must be visualized, beyond which alternate instruction will be called in, but it should be far enough from the median to take advantage of CAI's unique ability to deal with individual variance—up to a point.

All of the foregoing elements—corpus, objective and student set—need to be viewed within time. What will be the effect of growth and change? Can the CAI course be endowed with enough flexibility and dynamism to adjust? If not, is rapid write-off acceptable?

Lastly, the prospective author should have a clear idea as to whether instruction will be oriented primarily toward concepts or toward material to be memorized, whether it is problem-solving in nature or, rather, prerequisite to problem-solving. Each type presents its own particular challenge, and each calls for a different technical approach. Opinions differ as to the relative efficacy of CAI with respect to rote vs. conceptual material and with respect to problem-solving vs. something less creative. A reasonable policy would be to ask CAI to do nothing remarkable outside of the type of instruction usually provided in the lecture mode.

Now it is time to go back and examine each of the five elements in the light of the other four, in order to detect inconsistencies and to make appropriate adjustments. The whole should then be synthesized *in writing*, to produce an epitome that will withstand the shafts of one's own doubts and those of others. By referring to this statement frequently during the actual writing of the course, the author maintains a sense of balance and purpose without which his product will be erratic and incomplete. It may later become evident that the magnitude of the assumed task exceeds available resources, in which case one or the other needs to be modified. It is impossible to assess these things reliably ahead of time, especially if corpus needs to be completely over-hauled before it can be incorporated in CAI.

THE SYLLABUS

3.

THE SYLLABUS

CAI does some rather strange things to the conventional idea of *syllabus,* which we usually think of as a written outline purporting to indicate the extent of a course of instruction, to define its parts, and to suggest relationships between these parts. A syllabus announces a hierarchical structure of *presentation,* and usually tries to gear this structure to a schedule of classes and assignments. It is admittedly artificial and not very informative, but at least it satisfies the human urge to partition things and ideas. And it does serve the practical purpose of delimiting the instructor's and the student's area of responsibility. Whether it will be remembered for long, or if remembered will be of much use in a world of blurring boundaries, is another matter.

In addition to the conventional formal syllabus, one can

imagine at least four inchoate syllabi in a given transfer situation:

(1) The teacher's inner view of the structure of a subject.

(2) The teacher's view of how the structure should be expressed for transfer purposes.

(3) The student's understanding of (2).

(4) The student's ultimate view of the structure of the subject.

It seems reasonable to assert that (1) and (4) are what really count. If (2) is converted to a mimeographed handout, and if (3) is converted to student notes, it is possible for them to be so rigidly modelled that the student is inhibited from putting together, in (4)–according to his way of looking at things–an approximation of (1).

CAI in its more highly developed forms allows us to omit (2) and (3) altogether, because it permits presentation to be ordered according to student-generated patterns rather than according to a *single* teacher-imposed pattern. It does this by breaking up instruction into its smallest elements, which may then be manipulated and sequenced in a variety of ways by means of conditional branching and subroutines. The student's own condition determines his path through the subject, and eventually he will have woven an awareness of structure which is uniquely his own. It will doubtless differ from the teacher's concept of what it should be, because the student has started from a position of zero comprehension within corpus, whereas the teacher's version will have been based on whole comprehension.

Aside from this factor let us suppose that because of constraints within the subject matter itself the student's ultimate concept of structure is fairly close to that which the teacher would have imposed. The question is: is it more viable for the student, has it been learned more efficiently, and will it be remembered more vividly than if it had been imposed on him? If so, we might contemplate eliminating the formal syllabus altogether.

This would not mean the eclipse of the teacher's structural concept—only that it would manifest itself somewhat differently.

Computer operations are essentially linear ("DO this and then do this and then do this . . . ") rather than parallel-branching ("DO this and that, meanwhile deciding about the other . . . "). We speak of *branching* in programmed instruction, but a computer "sees" only one arm of a branch—the one it is told to follow—and has no awareness of the arms it is *not* following. Its track through the most complicated program could be pulled out in a straight line.

Turning to the root meaning of "syllabus"—as a "tied-together list"—it is possible to envisage a fairly close correspondence between it and the linear unfolding of a CAI program. We could, in fact, attach syllabus rubrics to the individual instructional elements, with the understanding that although their order might be somewhat altered, they would all be executed at some time during the running of the program.

The author can set up a list-type syllabus for this purpose, covering every foreseeable element of instruction as distinctly as possible, but without attaching particular importance to the sequencing of these elements *except* for those whose nature ties them imperatively to one another. In the latter case, where several elements are so closely bonded together that it is inconceivable that they would be approached in any way other than as a cluster, the cluster itself should be given a rubric.

A syllabus constructed in this way would look very much like a list-type syllabus, but its sequence would be understood to be provisional only. Later we shall see how its rubrics can be carried over into the actual coursewriting.

Some students depend heavily on landmarks. They become almost ill if they cannot continually reassure themselves as to where they are in relationship to a fixed program. (This probably comes from years of habit, marching from class to class, from subject to subject, and from school to school.) Recognizing that at least part of his student set will be so constituted, the author might plan to provide them with a rudimentary version of his working syllabus, with the understanding that their paths through it may diverge from the implied sequence.

BASIC TEXT

4.
BASIC TEXT

The CAI author's next step is to write a textbook!

The reason why text must be laid down in advance, *en bloc,* with great precision and attention to detail, is that almost every statement will be subject to intense scrutiny when the time comes to incorporate it into an instructional frame. A single word that is not quite right can throw a whole frame out of kilter. In lecturing, a teacher can often sense when one of his statements falls short of the mark, and he can rectify the fault immediately. An instructional statement in CAI must be almost monumentally clear. It should mean approximately the same thing to many different people, who may have cause to refer to it again and again. Some of these individuals will show an almost diabolical capacity for misunderstanding, and there will be no chance for them to consult together after class in order to straighten things out, because there will be no class.

The tone of the planned course can be foreshadowed in the initial text. Later on, when writing corrective and reinforcing responses, cues and so on, one can lighten a tone which might in itself be considered rather dry. So the basic text may safely be cast more formally than is planned for the ultimate effect.

The student will identify the course and the medium and to some extent even the subject matter with an imagined teacher whose *persona* is derived from a certain composite tone. About all the author can hope to convey of himself is an aura of reasonableness, patience, and understanding. Use of a homely expression now and then does no harm. The kind of helper-phrases which lubricate oral discourse should be used liberally, even though they carry little meaning and occupy valuable display space at the student terminal, because they are indispensable to the conversational mode. By the same token, statements which in a printed text might be admired for their elegance may alienate the type of student who is ill at ease amid too much perfection. Statements which are packed too tightly with meaning force him to stop and re-read more often than we would like him to.

One way to tackle the preparation of text would be to listen to tape recordings of one's own lectures, and then try to re-draft the same presentation from memory. Remedial sessions with individual students should also be taped, if possible. They will provide the author with a wealth of conversational gambits for use later on, together with an indication of elements in the starting corpus which he would be well advised to stress or to improve.

The author/instructor tries to avoid committing to CAI those portions of corpus which are threatened by change or controversy, preferring to handle them in a more agile medium. This stricture does not apply to simple updating, which can be accomplished with ease—particularly if items characteristically requiring such service are flagged in the system. On the other hand, even minor shifts in emphasis, approach, or aspect may take hours to implement. Whole frames may have to be rewritten or discarded and every associated mechanistic device may need to be checked and rechecked to ensure that no side-effect of the change has been overlooked.

One excellent hedge against the painful necessity of performing deep surgery on an existing program in order to win its acceptance is to engage one's associates in some of the early planning. One should seek the most candid criticism ahead of time, rather than waiting until all the work is done and the program is ready to go on-line. Even those who refuse to take CAI seriously will find it hard to keep aloof from the intrinsics of the subject to be taught. They can be asked to help hammer out the tougher definitions and to separate the ambiguities in the original block of text. Little by little these individuals may become intrigued by the whole idea of the project, and may even prove to be its staunchest supporters. Frankly, it may be a case of disarming the opposition by demonstrating that CAI—far from being a threat to the teaching profession—lets us really think about what we are trying to teach, in a rational and unhurried setting.

Whatever the style of presentation habitually favored by the author, the "textbook" now taking shape in his hands needs to be organized in such a way as to be amenable to the cut-and-paste operations ahead. Large glittering constructions must be avoided. Modest step-by-step progressions, the size of the steps being fairly uniform, are better suited to the medium. The text should be hospitable to examples, contrasts, hypothetical cases, and questions. Color, variety, movement, and humor are also needed, in order to compensate partly for the machine's lack of personal appeal and for the fact that unlike a teacher it cannot raise its voice or rap a lectern in order to emphasize a point.

A majority of cathode-ray terminals (CRTs) do not provide for underlining of words, or even for use of upper and lower case. One can separate the letters of words to be emphasized, but the effect is not particularly good. Some CRTs can cause a letter, a word, or a block of words to blink rapidly while the rest of the display remains steady. Quite possibly this could irritate the student beyond endurance.

After the author/instructor has finished drafting his textbook, it is time to tear it apart—literally, if he likes, as long as he keeps track of the pieces. A more orderly procedure is to go through the text bracketing major statements in colored pencil, then going through it again, bracketing minor statements in another color. The major statements should be delimited as naturally as possible. Well-reasoned accuracy should be the goal; one shouldn't worry too much about brevity.

To return to the major statements, the ones which need to be identified first:

These should be capable of standing alone, even worthy of being memorized. The object is to present a complete, well-rounded concept *accurately*. Most CRT systems provide simultaneous display of some 1000 characters. With this much scope, an author can say something quite complicated, if he needs to, and say it well. In addition, many CRTs have two or three times as much space on the screen as is needed for their total number of characters, so that text may be liberally formatted without loss of character capacity.

One thing which stops instruction in its tracks is a statement which leaves nothing more to be said, like the old lady's reply when asked if she were related to a well known Philadelphia family, "No—they are related to me." If a major statement is brought to a thunderous conclusion, it seems almost frivolous to ask a student to comment on it. One or two loose ends—a sense of " . . . and so . . . and then . . . ," a sense of interesting ramifications to be explored—give author and student a chance to continue reasoning together.

Turning to "minor statements," for which "satellite statements" might be a better term, it may be observed that these fall naturally into two groups:

Group 1. Those which reinforce or elaborate upon ideas advanced in major statements, and in combination with the latter make up the clusters we referred to in the previous chapter, and

Group 2. Those which serve to provide transition between main groupings (the nodes or "rubrics" in the linear syllabus).

The author may wish to distinguish between the two in marking up his basic text.

The next step is to key the minor statements to the major statements to which they principally relate. Those having multiple relationships should be keyed accordingly. The instructional network will ultimately consist of hundreds of these syndetic ties.

Normally a transition statement will immediately precede a major statement. If missing from this position, the reason may be that the major statement is so highly consequent of its predecessor that transition can be established in an opening phrase. Later, if entry from another part of the program is desired, this function may have to be expanded.

Throughout this bracketing and tagging process the author will be wondering how on earth he is going to bring the student on-stage and keep him there.

(1) He can approach the problem in a purely catechismic way, as to say, "Well, after telling the student ABC, I will turn around and ask him to tell *me* ABC."

(2) Or he can open things up by the approach, "I'll tell the student AB and find out if he understands by requiring him to invert it (BA), or furnish an example (AB_{xpl}) or exception (AB_{xpt})." It need hardly be said that the creative or quasi-creative demands imposed on the student by the latter approach constitute far better pedagogy. (They make the pedagogue work harder, too.)

(3) Another way to regard a statement is to ask one's self, "What might a student with an active, exploring mind ask about this? What relationships might he (correctly or incorrectly) deduce? What implications (supportable or not) might occur to him?" This approach requires a great deal of imagination. It also demands poise—the courage and understanding to grope around in limbo. The author must not only contemplate faulty logic; he must invent it!

Each of these three approaches will prove more appropriate than the other two, at various times. Even the first has its uses, mostly mechanical. The second is the workhorse of the three. The third offers the greatest challenge.

FRAMES

5.

FRAMES

The author/instructor now prepares to embark upon the actual writing of frames. From this point onward, his work will be subject to the special requirements of the CAI medium.

The word "frame" means essentially the same thing for CAI as it does for a programmed text: a teaching statement subjoined by a question and student answer space, followed by program reaction to student answer. The similarity does not go much beyond this characterization, because

1. With a programmed text, only the statement, the question, and the program reaction are displayed to the student, while with CAI the student's own answer is displayed as well (Figure 1).

2. With programmed text the number and nature of

FIGURE 1

A. *Page of programmed text*
(p. 42 in "An Introduction to the Sears List of Subject Headings" by Philip R.D. Corrigan (Series title: A Programmed Text in Library and Information Science, C.D. Batty, ed., London: Clive Bingley, 1967.)

48. The time has now come to construct subject headings and references using Sears. Using what we have learned about the structure of Sears, you should be able to choose headings. If, for example, you were asked to construct a heading for the document "Children and Television" you should arrive at

TELEVISION AND CHILDREN.

The phrase CHILDREN AND TELEVISION is a reference in Sears.

Now construct a heading for a document on stamp collecting.

POSTAGE STAMPS	71
PHILATELY	86
STAMP COLLECTING	74

(p. 71, Ibid.)

---

49. Good. Now, given that the subject heading for a document

    Furniture manufacture

    is FURNITURE

    give the headings used for the *see also* references needed for this book.

    ART, DECORATIVE

    ART OBJECTS

    DECORATION AND ORNAMENT

    HOME ECONOMICS

    INTERIOR DECORATION

    MANUFACTURES*   If all see page 61

    UPHOLSTERY*   If only those marked*

    WOODWORK*   see page 82

(Note that "Good" would represent program reaction in a CAI frame, and the remainder of p.71 is really a new frame.)

(p. 86, Ibid.)

48A Not quite, the correct heading is POSTAGE
STAMPS. PHILATELY means stamp collecting
and it is in Sears but only as a reference. Headings
in light type are NOT used as subject headings.

Construct a subject heading for a book on the Post
Office.

POST OFFICE   54

POSTAL SERVICE   71

(Note that all of the first paragraph would be
considered program reaction in CAI.)

(p. 74, Ibid.)

48B No. You are simply using the title, which is NOT in
Sears. STAMPS, POSTAGE is in Sears as a reference and would have led you to the correct
heading: POSTAGE STAMPS.

Construct a heading for the document *Book
collecting.*

BOOKS - COLLECTING   54

BOOK COLLECTING   71

(Again, the first paragraph constitutes program reaction. Note also that reactions to the choices in new "sub"-frames 48A and 48B are identical.)

B. *Successive displays (CRT) in a CAI program*
   (Portions of the same material as above, re-cast.)

The time has now come to construct subject headings and references using Sears. You should be able to choose headings based on what you have learned of the structure of the Sears List. For example, for a book entitled "Children and Television" you should arrive at

TELEVISION AND CHILDREN.

The phrase CHILDREN AND TELEVISION is indicated as a reference *to* TELEVISION AND CHILDREN.

Now please construct a heading for a document on stamp collecting.

The same display, after the student has typed his answer:

The time has now come to construct subject headings and references using Sears. You should be able to choose headings based on what you have learned of the structure of the Sears List. For example, for a book entitled "Children and Television" you should arrive at

TELEVISION AND CHILDREN.

The phrase CHILDREN AND TELEVISION is indicated as a reference *to* TELEVISION AND CHILDREN.

Now please construct a heading for a document on stamp collecting.

PHILATELY

The display after the student has pressed the "send block" key:

Not quite. Headings in light type are NOT used as subject headings. The word PHILATELY appears in Sears only as a reference, not as a heading. Try another term.

The student would then try again, his response appearing below the text as in the preceding display.

(End of Figure 1.)

different program reactions are severely limited, whereas CAI can be made to react in a great number and variety of ways.

That part of a CAI frame which a student sees may look exactly like a page from a programmed text, but back in the computer whole platoons of instructions will have been mustered to govern program reaction to his awaited input. If all these instructions were written out in plain language for the student to follow, he would be inundated. They are usually seen only by the author/instructor, the encoder, the keypuncher, and the computer itself. The computer ingests and compiles the total course, and produces a printed version for future reference.

A computer executes a CAI program (i.e., interacts with on-line input from a student) by virtue of a special programming device which forces it to stop and do nothing—absolutely nothing—at a specified point in each frame. This point is marked by a code of some kind, which is said to throw the computer into "wait" condition. It remains in this condition while the student types out an answer. When the answer is complete, the student signals the fact that he is ready for the computer to consider it, usually by pressing a single key such as the "send" button on his terminal keyboard.

The computer then seizes the student's input and rushes off* to compare it with one or more words (or letters or

* It is hard to say much about computers without personalizing them now and then.

numbers or symbols) which it has been instructed to look for in that particular frame. If it achieves a "match," that is, if something in a student response corresponds exactly with something the computer has been told to look for, it sets a decision-switch and goes on to do what it has been told to do, under that condition. Otherwise, it does what it has been told to do in case the decision switch is *not* set. Either way, a new display to the student will probably be called forth—something pertinent to the student's response if it has been matched; something more general if all match attempts have failed—followed by a return to the waiting mode for a "try again" or by passing to the next frame.

Always the computer is looking for the next thing to do, and only the code saying, "Wait! Give the student a chance to talk!" makes it sit back and cool its heels.

The proper codes for this and all other operations governing the execution of a CAI course can be added *after* the author has completed the major part of his work, including the actual design of frames, the writing of display statements, and the specification of elements which the computer is to try to match against student input.

Codes vary according to different CAI languages, and not all languages (nor the systems in which they are intended to be implemented) will do the same things in the same way. But in most cases the same *type* of operations will take place in any of the "high-level conversational" languages, such as those Frye designates "Group IV—Special Instructional" (Frye, 1968). The point I hope to make in this manual is that the author need not ascertain in advance the particular language to be employed, before proceeding with his part of the work.

In the execution of a program, computer operations tend to follow the same sequence as that in which they were compiled, except when a command to jump to another part of the program is encountered. This jumping around is done easily and (almost) instantly, but always an address to jump *to* is needed, and we call this address a *label.* Labels can be attached to a number of different things—display statements, wait modes, commands—in such a way as to make them accessible from anywhere in the program.

Not everything needs to be labelled—only those items which are to be jumped to, or will be used in some other way, such as quoting their contents. Certainly the display statements which begin a frame need to be labelled, not only because they are frequently jumped to from other parts of the program, but also because they need to be related to rubrics in the syllabus. It is a good idea to distinguish frame labels in some way, such as by attaching a dot-alpha suffix to a mnemonic. For instance, if this paragraph were to be re-cast into three CAI frames, we might label them

LABEL.A
LABEL.B
LABEL.C

Suppose we build a simple frame around a very simple statement/question:

Frame label:	GENUS. A
Statement:	(Assume display of expository text.)

Question	On what kind of trees do oranges grow?
Wait mode	(Imagine student input here, ending with a signal turning operation back to the computer.)
Look for match with	Citron.

(program reaction)

Display statement	You are very close, but "citron" is another example of the same genus. Try changing the word slightly.
Look for match with	Citrus aurantium.
Display statement	Excellent! You are remarkably well informed.
Look for match with	Citrus.
Display statement	Correct.

Look for match with	Orange.
Display statement	Yes, yes, but what genus covering not only orange trees but lemon, lime and grapefruit trees as well?
Fail-match display statement No. 1	I mean what genus—corresponding, for example, with "conifers" for pine trees?
Fail-match display statement No. 2	The answer is "citrus."

(next frame follows)

Unless directed otherwise, the computer will perform all of the above steps in sequence and fall through to the next frame. Obviously, some special instructions are needed, namely commands to jump back to waiting mode after either of the two "wrong" matches and also after Fail-match No. 1. To jump anywhere, the destination must be specified, so we must label both the wait mode and the beginning of the next frame with some kind of address, say "KUMQUAT" and "ONWARD. A" respectively.

Also suppose we adopt two-letter codes to indicate the types of operation involved instead of writing them out in full each time:

DS...   Display statement

WM..   Wait Mode

SS....   Scan specification ("look for match with")

DO ..   *Do* something

FM ..   Fail-match display statement

The frame will then look like this:

GENUS. A	DS	(expository statement, followed by:) On what kind of trees do oranges grow?
KUMQUAT	WM	_____
	SS	Citron.
	DS	You are very close, but "citron" is another example of the same genus. Try changing the word slightly.
	DO	Jump to KUMQUAT.
	SS	Citrus aurantium.
	DS	Excellent! You are remarkably well informed.

DO   Jump to ONWARD.A.

SS   Citrus.

DS   Correct.

DO   Jump to ONWARD.A.

SS   Orange.

DS   Yes, yes, but what genus cov-
                      ering not only orange trees but
                      lemon, lime and grapefruit
                      trees as well?

DO   Jump to KUMQUAT.

DO   Check to see if FM No. 1 has
                      been used yet. If so, skip it.

FM No. 1   I mean what genus . . . cor-
                      responding, for example, with
                      "conifers" for pine trees?

DO   Make a note that FM No. 1
                      has been used once, then jump
                      to KUMQUAT.

FM No. 2   The answer is "citrus."

(The DO jump to ONWARD.A is unnecessary here, because ONWARD.A is the next item in sequence.)

ONWARD.A   DS   (Beginning of next frame)

The DS and DO codes are still not quite right, because for the most part we want them to operate only under certain conditions. So the foregoing example could be refined by letting "DSM" stand for a display statement which would appear to the student only if a match had been obtained on the SS immediately preceding. The same stipulation could apply to "DOM." We could use "DOF" to mean "do only in case of fail-match." Just plain DO could then be used to mean "do this in any case, if you ever get to this point instead of jumping over it."

Try marking the above example accordingly, then check to see if the codes as amended occur in the following order: DS, WM, SS, DSM, DOM, SS, DSM, DOM, SS, DSM, DOM, SS, DSM, DOM, DO, FM No. 1, DOF, FM No. 2, DS.

THE WORKSHEET

6.

THE WORKSHEET

The running text will soon be so heavily marked with brackets and arrows and dotted lines and keynumbers that it would be expedient to copy the whole thing out in expanded form—something like the "exploded drawings" used to depict intricate machinery to the layman. For this a special form is needed, a form which can display all the materials and operations which the author desires to incorporate in his course. The form should make his intentions clear both to himself and to others, particularly to the person who will be doing the encoding.

Figure 2 shows the form of coding sheet we have found to be highly successful for this purpose. Its virtue lies in the fact that the various commands are separated from the textual display items with which they are for the most part concerned. This makes it possible to review the instruction itself, in the sequence which would occur if no review or enrichment subroutines were involved, without having to read through a clutter of program machinery. The "machinery" is worked-up in the right-hand column directly opposite the text material to which it relates.

This worksheet will be the interface between the author and the coder, after the author has pushed it through several drafts to the point where it represents what he wants to do. If he wishes, the author can indicate his intentions in plain English. He is under no obligation to adhere to anyone's code. As he proceeds, however, he will find himself improvising symbols as a kind of shorthand for the operations he wants the coder to implement. This is fine, as long as he disciplines himself to adhere to certain rules:

1. Each operation (including textual display) must have an instruction or symbol attached to it.
2. Each instruction or symbol must mean one and only one specific thing to be done.
3. Each instruction symbol must fall into executable sequence.

The first of these rules is required so that nothing will drift around in the program unattached to *some* operational command. Even display statements need to be preceded by a code of some kind, saying "print me now," or they will fail to appear when wanted, or even worse will reel out when *not* wanted, like a bibulous aunt during the parson's first call. One cannot leave the matter up to the coder, because he needs to be told (among other things) whether a display is to occur invariably or conditionally.

For example, the author may want to use a response statement such as "No, a 'tempest in a teapot' is not a meteorological phenomenon. It is a figure of speech." *only* if the student's input deserves it, or "Not understood. Please rephrase." *only* if the student has said something the author has failed to anticipate or has considered to be not worth making special provision for. These two conditions need to be specified to be executed; otherwise, the program will cause every display statement to be executed when encountered, whether the statement makes sense or not.

The second requirement, that each symbol means one and only one thing to be done, reflects the computer's basic simple-mindedness. An important corollary is that the computer will try to do the same thing to all objects placed before it, while following out a particular command. This characteristic can be exploited. For example, suppose the author wants to add one digit to each of three variables—such as three different scoring tallies—and let "DO" represent the command "do the following:" He *could* write it out DO ADD 1 TO ASCORE, DO ADD 1 TO BSCORE, DO ADD 1 TO CSCORE. But all he really needs is the one command DO ADD 1 TO ASCORE, BSCORE, CSCORE.

Again, the above codes are for example only. The author can use *any notation he fancies.* He might, in fact, combine the "DO" and "ADD" into a single predicate, like "DADD." However, there is a drawback to this, because the

FIGURE 2

Sample Worksheet

		DISPLAY TEXT AND SCAN SPECIFICATIONS		COMMANDS	
LABELS	CODES	OPERANDS	CODES	OPERANDS	

"DO" part will often need to be conditional, i.e., qualified so that it will operate only when a certain condition exists, such as a successful match between the student's input and the author's scan specification. This rather overloads a single code, because then each code would have three elements: (1) the precondition requirement, (2) the action imperative, and (3) the type of action to be taken.

The third requirement, that symbols must be ordered in executable sequence, has to be met scrupulously if the author expects his program to work the way he wants it to. Suppose he has written something like "DO JUMP TO REVIEW.A" at a point where he wants the student to be diverted, or "jumped," to another part of the instruction—which he has labeled REVIEW.A. Later it occurs to him that he should have the computer keep a record of the number of times the student is thus branched, so he tacks on "DO ADD 1 TO REVIEWAT. (being the label of this one record) thus:

DO JUMP TO REVIEW.A, DO ADD 1 TO REVIEWAT

What's wrong? The first command will be executed as soon as it is understood by the computer; the second command might just as well not exist! Correct sequence calls for reversing their order. This looks painfully obvious; but when the going gets thick, the rule can easily be overlooked.

Whether one writes everything out in longhand or develops his own private notation, it is the better part of valor to be prodigal in leaving room for changes and insertions. This practice minimizes the dull and dangerous business of transcribing the material more often than is absolutely necessary.

We have seen how the author sets about entering his material in systematic form so that a coder can interpret his wishes and convert them to a form acceptable to the computer. I suggested writing out text in the left-hand side of the form, with the corresponding operational commands on the right. Now, I want to discuss another type of entry which should also go on the left-hand side, along with the text: the *scan specifications*, which indicate which words or letters or numerals the student's input must contain in order to satisfy a prerequisite to some program response or action.

A specification might look like this (assume "SS" to mean "scan for:")

SS   RICHARD NIXON

following a question such as "Who in 1968 was elected President of the United States?" Or it might be written

SS   NIXON

or even

SS   NIX*   (see footnote)

(Note: The asterisk is used as a convention herein, replacing any and all unspecified characters.)

All three would probably match some part of a correct answer, with little danger of matching an incorrect answer. If a match condition with the scan is achieved, the program could provide for the display of something like

CORRECT

Scan specifications are the heart of the program, just as main statements may be said to be the heart of the instruction. The art and science of scan design will be dealt with later. For the present, it is unnecessary for the reader to think about it in any but the simplest terms. This is so that he may concentrate on the next major step, which is to start asking questions about the substance of the corpus.

QUESTIONS

7.

QUESTIONS

Earlier, in describing the process of breaking up basic text into manageable pieces which could be discussed with the student, I advocated that the statements themselves be chosen and worded in such a way as to lend themselves to this treatment.

Various writers have dealt with question design for all kinds of purposes and all kinds of media, including the writing of frames for programmed textbooks (Frye, 1968). Rather than trudge through this material, let us look briefly at those elements which set CAI question-technique somewhat apart:

There are two major differences:

1.   The CAI medium permits the instructor to deal uniquely with each of several answers to the same question.

2. The CAI medium permits the instructor to deal with a great number of *variant* responses as if they were identical, provided an author-specified *something* appears in the response. Essentially this means that the program forgives or ignores all extraneous matter, and the student can word his responses any way he wants to as long as he uses the words called for in the scan specification.

The first of these allows the instructor to open out the scope of his questions. In a programmed text, the student is usually restricted to two or three choices in answering a question, because of the physical limitation on textbook size and complexity. In CAI no such limit exists. The question might be, for example: "Name four 19th Century American novelists." To this question we could append dozens of separate scan specifications, such as:

SS   STOWE
DSM   Yes, Harriet Beecher Stowe was one of them.

SS   HENRY JAMES
DS   No. Although Henry James was born in the U.S., he expatriated himself very early in his career, and is generally considered an English author.

SS   SINCLAIR LEWIS
DSM   Sorry, wrong century. Sinclair Lewis' first novel ('Our Mr. Wren') was published in 1913.

Let us consider the same example to illustrate the second elementary difference noted above. Suppose the student, in answer to the question, wrote:

	I think that Harriet B. Stowe was one.
or	Stowe, H.B.
or	Was it Stowe?

In each case the scan specification "STOWE" would have been successfully matched.

The significance of this is that CAI opens up whole new vistas of communication with the student by permitting him to express himself naturally. This potential should be taken advantage of at every opportunity, even though it means a great deal more effort on the part of the author/instructor. It encourages the student to see through the computer to the very human teacher on the other side of the electronic device. The results seem to be an enhancement of the learning process, perhaps because spontaneity—even simulated spontaneity—is an apparently strong motivational factor (Gordon, 1969; Stolurow, 1968).

The form of the question, or, rather, the form of the answer which an author tries to elicit by his question, should be varied to suit the circumstances. The author should exercise certain preferences of form, whenever possible, in order to give fullest play to the natural language level of instruction.

Accordingly, questions that can be answered in the affirmative or negative are preferable to true-false types, since the latter embody a certain stiffness and artificiality in both the question and its answer.

Heavily formatted questions are especially weak: they break the conversational style, and in addition erect in the student's mind secondary problems of performance quite apart from the gist of the instruction.

If a multiple choice question is offered, the choices should be presented in plain language *without* key-numbers or key-letters.

If a missing word is to be supplied in a constructed-response type of question, let it be at the end of the statement, since that is where most dialogical interruptions occur.

After working in the CAI medium for some time, and observing the response patterns of many students, a programmer can broaden the scope of his elicited responses. Initially, however, he should frame his questions rather narrowly in order to attain a reasonable probability that student responses will match one of his scan specifications.

What this reasonable probability is, it is difficult to say. It fluctuates with question substance and the instructional level. If a set of scans in a particular frame fails to snare more than half of the student responses on the first pass, it is likely either that the question should be altered or that the scans should be re-worked. If operational experience indicates the other extreme, i.e., match probability *too* high, perhaps the question should be opened up.

Although I have emphasized amenability of the instructional text to a broad question-answer mode, it would be awkward to try to imagine all likely responses for each frame at the same time. In particular, it would tend to obscure the flow of thought which the author is trying to attain. Rather, one should write minimal dialogue until the whole structure begins to take shape.

Conjure up, if you will, an ideal student—one who always understands what you have told him and remembers it with perfect accuracy. Let him be your "straight man," and write him alone into the first draft. Let his perfect answers provide your lead to a reinforcing statement whenever possible, rather than simply saying "Correct" and pushing him into the next frame.*

Having satisfied himself that his dialogue with the perfect student is pedagogically sound, has a good "story line," makes the student think for himself, covers the subject

---

*It has been suggested that the quickest, brightest students should receive some special enrichment during the running of the program, this extra measure to be doled out on the basis of high tallies recorded within the program. But the *minimal* student *does* get through the course, finally, by virtue of elaborate branching, corrective routines, drill-and-practice, and so on. After all this *sturm und drang* doesn't he deserve enrichment too? If the corpus is organically sound and everyone gets through it, enrichment for the few seems unfair. Such material belongs in the basic instruction if it belongs in the course at all.

without obliterating it, and takes advantage of the conversational mode as much as possible, the author turns to deal with the other members of his student set. Henceforth, he will be like a dramatic producer presiding over an especially unruly cast of characters, none of whom has a copy of the script. He must coax them along in spite of their aberrations, trying not to lose any of his players before the end of the last act.

ANSWERS

8.

ANSWERS

If one passes directly from question-asking to the specifying of scans against which to test student answers, it is a little like trying to snare rabbits with no clear idea of what a rabbit looks like. In this chapter an attempt will be made to characterize various types of answers which a student is capable of making, in such a way as to provide a good basis for individual scan design.

For each question we assume a set of "legal" answers, defined as answers containing at least one term (numeral, letter, symbol, English word or phrase) directly relevant to the question or its context. We further assume, for practical purposes, that:

1. Only that portion of an answer which does not overflow system limits will be considered for legality.

2. The order of elements in a legal answer must be syntactically sound (i.e., MAN BITES DOG, not BITES MAN DOG.) .

3. The author has cognizance of relevant terms.

The first two are self-evident. The third means that although the author will probably not imagine, initially, all the terms relevant to a question, some of these will be suggested later through operational experience, and the author will at that later time choose those to be added to the set of known legal terms. (The full set may never be known.)

Standard function words are relevant: positives, negatives, expressions of doubt, etc. These can be handled quite economically by storing their variants centrally and then referring to them by label instead of writing them out in full for each frame.

A convenient way of envisaging student answers is to let A represent the set of all possible statements a student might type into a line of maximum legal length. Then A_{Legal} is the set of "legal answers," and $A_{Illegal}$ is the set of all others. Thus $A_L + A_I = A$.

Not all A_L in response to a fairly open question can be perceived ahead of time. Let A_{LP} represent those which can be and are. The remainder are designated A_{LU} (unperceived). After operational testing begins, some A_{LU} will move over to A_{LP}.

Not all A_{LP} are dealt with by the author according to their meaning. Some will occur so seldom, or the extraction of their meaning by the program will be so complicated, that the effort of providing for them uniquely would be excessive. Accordingly they are handled as if they had no meaning; we permit them to be dumped into the "FAIL" hopper along with the A_I and the A_{LU}, whence they are either processed through a "try again" loop or otherwise disposed of. We can call this type "Failed-A_{LP}" or A_{LPF}, and let F represent all failed A, such that $F = A_{LPF} + A_{LU} + A_I$.

This lets us define all answers which will *not* be failed (answers containing terms which will be recognized as relevant, and for which the author will make specific provision) as "Match-A_{LP}," or A_{LPM}.

There are three types of A_{LPM}: those that are "right" according to the author; those that are "wrong" in the sense of being exactly the opposite of right; and those that are neither right nor wrong in this reciprocal sense. The last group may be intermediate or peripheral in a number of ways. They may be unclear to the system or even to the human author apart from the system. But in any case the author believes them to be worth discussing.

To Illustrate:

Question: Who is President: Nixon or Johnson?

Answer.1   Nixon A_{LPM}-Right

Answer.2   Johnson A_{LPM}-Wrong

Answer.3   Do you mean President of U.S.? A_{LPM}-Other

Answer.4   I'm not sure. A_{LPM}-Other

Answer.5   Not Johnson. A_{LPM}-Other

Answer.6   The one with a dog "Checkers." A_{LPF}

Answer.7   Head of Republican Party. A_{LU}*

Answer.8   Eisenhower's vice. A_I

Answer.9   I'm hungry. A_I

*(assume concealed from the author until after operational experience.)

The category which gives us the most trouble is A_{LPM}-Other, so let us examine the various conditions which singly or in combination give rise to this kind of answer.

1.   One or more elements of the instructional statement unclear.

2.   One or more elements of the question unclear.

                                    (Answer.3)

3.   Student preparation faulty.

                                    (Answer.4)

4. Student has forgotten earlier instruction.

5. Student has missed a transition.

6. Student mistrusts a question, seeks a recondite meaning.

7. Student thinks he sees a fallacy in the question.

8. Student thinks he sees an exception to a rule.

9. Student objects to something in the underlying statement ("point-of-order").

10. Student objects to something in question ("point-of-order").

11. Student is curious to see what will be said in response to a wild or contrary answer.

(Answer.5)

12. Student is hurt or angry.

A more extended example will show how these conditions can result in a veritable Pandora's box of responses, all ALPM, ALPF, or ALU:

Statement: In Pliny one is told of 2-cubit unicorn horns.
Question: How many horns has a unicorn?

In response to this very faulty combination we can imagine at least some A$_{LPM}$-Other as:

(Condition)

Were the unicorns 2 cubits long or their horns?	1
It means a mythical beast.	2
Where's Pliny?	3,4,5
What's a unicorn? I never studied biology.	3,4,5
Zero. Unicorn = nonexistent = zero.	
Therefore each of his parts = zero.	6
Either 1, or in the case of the Hebrew re-em, two.	7,8
You only said what Pliny said. What are the facts?	9
I hate trick questions.	10
Same as monocerus.	11
Really!	12

The number of possible variations on this set could run into the hundreds. We could undertake to accommodate them all, but it makes more sense to rework the statement/question, improving it in ways that will minimize *unproductive* A$_{LPM}$, to wit, those which fail to lead to any enhancement of the instruction. Most of those in the horrible example above can be so described.

A *productive* A$_{LPM}$, on the other hand, is one to which the computer can respond in a genuinely instructive vein. "Zero. Unicorn = nonexistent. . . " (above) might so qualify, because the author could respond by saying that although the unicorn itself may be nonexistent the same does not apply to the *unicorn idea*—and lead the student back to the question.

Much as we would like all A$_{LPM}$-Other to be productive, no amount of precision and care in assembling the statement/question will rule out the other kind, because we have no final control over the conditions listed above.

Suppose we are able to reduce unproductive A$_{LPM}$ satisfactorily by tidying up the instruction and the question. What about all the possible variants in productive A$_{LPM}$— same ideas differently worded? Fortunately, these do not all need to be specified by the author. It will be enough for him to indicate the basic ideas clearly to the coder in the hope that it will be technically feasible for the latter to provide the necessary mechanisms for detecting them in a host of forms.

This is a good place to bring the coder into the picture, in an effort to find out exactly what he needs in the way of explicit instructions from the author in order to put the course in machine-executable form.

MECHANISMS

9.

MECHANISMS

In speaking of the coder we have in mind not only the person who will labor over the author/instructor's programmatical output. We think also of the underlying hardware and software which make up the system in which the CAI course is to be implemented. The author/instructor will probably deal with programmers and system designers as well as the coder, but generally we can consider all these elements as a single entity, with the coder as their interface with the author.

As indicated in the Introduction, the purpose of this book is to show a teacher how he may start putting together a CAI course before a complete system for implementing it is placed on his doorstep. It has been pointed out that a teacher's insistence on certain system characteristics carries a great deal of weight with designers and programmers, and should be voiced early and distinctly.

This does not mean the prospective CAI author, drunk with power, may demand things beyond the scope of computer technology as it now exists. Everyone operates under some constraint or other, and it is well for the author to be aware of things he cannot—in 1971—expect a computer to do. The computer cannot be as perceptive as a human teacher. It doesn't really "understand" a string of words for which it has not been amply programmed in advance. But on balance there are so many things a computer can do, and can do very well, that effective CAI is indeed within our grasp.

I have previously mentioned scan specifications in connection with the use of the worksheet. Now we must consider them more closely, because they are, as I have said, the heart of the system.

Let us start with a fresh example:

QUESTION: What Irishman wrote the play from which 'My Fair Lady' was adapted?

Answer.1   It was George Bernard Shaw. A_{LPM}-Right

Answer.2   Shaw, I think. A_{LPM}-Right

Answer.3   The redoubtable G.B.S. A_{LPM}-Right

Answer.4   Loewe. A_{LPM}-Other

Answer.5   Lerner. A_{LPM}-Other

Answer.6   Rex Harrison. A_{LPM}-Other

Answer.7   The author of 'Pygmalion.' A_{LPM}-Other

Answer.8   What is 'My Fair Lady' about? A_{LPM}-Other

Answer.9   I thought 'My Fair Lady' was a musical.
                                                         A_{LPM}-Other

Answer.10   The one with the red beard. A_{LPF}

Answer.11   I'm not sure. A_{LPM}-Other

Answer.12   Can't remember. A_{LPM}-Other

Answer.13   _____(unperceived)
                                                         A_{LU}

Answer.14   _____(illegal) A_I

A scan specification identical with Answer.1, "It was George Bernard Shaw," would most certainly effect a successful match. But if the student said just "George Bernard Shaw" the match attempt on such a scan would fail, and the author's intention be defeated. Since *George Bernard Shaw* is the essential element of this particular A_{LPM}, the author should underline (in this text they will appear italicized) those words to indicate to the coder that everything else may be omitted from the scan specification *if* the coder can do this without opening the door to unwanted matches.

The author then proceeds to write a statement to be displayed to the student if any part of the student's input matches the specification, something like "Correct. Shaw's 'Pygmalion,' first produced in 1913, was based on the Greek legend of the sculptor . . . (etc.)" Suppose we label this statement ELIZA.1 and insert it in the proper sequence following the scan to be matched.

Question:	What Irishman wrote the play from which 'My Fair Lady' was adapted?

Answer.1   It was *George Bernard Shaw.* A_{LPM}-Right

Eliza.1   Correct. Shaw's 'Pygmalion,' first produced in 1913, was based on the Greek legend of the sculptor . . . (etc.)

Answer.2   Shaw, I think. A_{LPM}-Right

Answer.3   The redoubtable G.B.S. A_{LPM}-Right

But wait! Couldn't ELIZA.1 serve as response to Answer.2 and Answer.3 as well? Yes it could. However, the author may first want to make sure whether the student knows Shaw's full name, and, if not, to tell him. This calls for its own separate scan, which will look for the single word *Shaw* in case the student says anything like Answer.2. The response to this might be "Yes, but please give his full name." Exactly the same treatment works for "The redoubtable G.B.S." so that we can combine the two scan specifications, thus:

Answer.2/Answer.3 *Shaw*, I think or The redoubtable *G.B.S.*

which might be written more compactly:

Answer.23   Shaw/G.B.S.   (any agreed symbol
representing the "or"-sign)

This would be followed by

Eliza.23   Yes, but please give his full name.

(Eliza.23 may have created a subordinate problem, to which we will return after looking at the remaining possible answers.)

Answer.4, Answer.5 and Answer.6 seem to call for something better than "Wrong. Try again," because each contains an item of valid information about 'My Fair Lady' which the teacher should be pleased to confirm:

Eliza.4   Frederick Loewe wrote the music for 'My Fair
Lady.' Alan Jay Lerner wrote the book for it. . .

Eliza.5   Alan Jay Lerner wrote the book for 'My Fair
               Lady.' Frederick Loewe wrote the music. . .

Eliza.6   Rex Harrison played the part of Professor Henry
               Higgins in the Broadway production and later in
               the film version. . .

adding identical cues to each:

> . . . The musical was adapted from 'Pygmalion,'
> which was written by the same man who wrote
> 'Back to Methuselah' and 'Major Barbara,' name-
> ly _____(?)

Rather than writing out this cue for all three, the author will
decide to give it a label—such as DRAMATIST and quote it
when needed.

Luckily DRAMATIST alone fits Answer.7 quite nicely,
so we can use it as a response to that answer as well.

Passing to Answer.8, it appears that the student is
inadequately prepared for the question, even though he may
be acquainted with the Pygmalion story and Shaw. A scan
based on the words MY FAIR LADY and the question mark
could detect this condition with reasonable efficiency, even
though a few unwanted A_L might also be snared in the
process. The teacher can try to bring this student up to parity
with:

Eliza.8   The theme of both 'My Fair Lady' and 'Pygma-
           lion,' the play on which it is based, is derived
           from the Greek story of a sculptor . . . (etc.) . . .
           with a secondary theme dealing with linguistics
           . . . (etc.)

Answer.9 can be scanned for MY FAIR LADY plus
MUSICAL but the results will not be very conclusive. All we
really know is that the student has made a statement in
which he used these terms but which does *not* fit any of the
preceding scans. The safest course is to respond with a
general statement about the musical, the movie and the
original play and hope for the best. This is better than
throwing the answer into the "Failed" hopper along with
unperceived and illegal answers (A_{LU} and A_I).

Answer.10 occurred to me as the sort of response a
student might make in rummaging for a fact which temporarily eluded him. It is a scrapbook item, hardly worth
considering. Perhaps no one else would think of it. Yet it has
excellent mnemonic qualities, and we have need of such
"handles." However, it is better to provide them in text
statements, actively, rather than passively in scan specifications which may never be used.

Accordingly, Answer.10 is treated as A_{LPF}: one which
the author perceives as a possibility somewhat too remote to
merit being assigned a unique scan specification and response
to fit.

Answer.11 and Answer.12, on the other hand, are of the type which often *does* merit unique response. Scan specifications for this type of answer can be detailed separately and stored under distinctive labels, such as NEGAT, POSIT, NOTHINK, YESTHINK and DOUBTFUL. We could scan for both simply by quoting the label DOUBTFUL, then using a responding statement which seems to acknowledge the fact that the student *is* doubtful. Let us put this one on the shelf temporarily, along with Eliza.23 (above) and return to them later.

The statements made in reply to answers falling into the "F" category (e.g., Answer.13 and Answer.14) often resemble those made to A_{LPM}-Other answers, but they need to be even more carefully worded. For one thing, they should avoid implying to the student that his input has been understood, when this is obviously untrue. Rather, the programmed response to an "F" answer needs to be couched in positive, forward-looking terms of clarification. "Wrong. Try again" by itself turns CAI into a guessing game of little pedagogical value. On the other hand "Try again" accompanied by a hint, or even by a complete restatement of the question, continues the instruction at the proper level.

It is possible to keep a student looping indefinitely through a frame, but this is hardly recommended. The correct answer should seldom be withheld through more than one or two complete failures.

"F" responses can be nested so that the first will be

used the first time through, the second on the second pass, and so on. If the question is quite an open one, or if the context is particularly rich in associative terms, the first F response should try to get the student to use some alternate wording, so that his next answer will have a better chance of being matched by some scan specification. The second should cue him very strongly, even asking a helping question, the answer to which will be, in fact, almost a guarantee of a match somewhere along the line. The third F response should normally furnish the answer. If the situation at this point is desperate enough, the student can be branched into a separate corrective routine, or he can be told to sign off and seek counsel before proceeding any further.

The following might be suitable F responses for the frame we have been struggling with:

ELIZA.F   Sorry, I missed your meaning. Please re-word your answer.

ELIZA.FF   You may remember him as the author of 'Pygmalion,' 'Man and Superman,' and 'The Intelligent Woman's Guide to Socialism and Capitalism'—a sort of perennial enfant terrible of English letters in the first decades of this century.

ELIZA.FFF   It was George Bernard Shaw . . .

Here, with ELIZA.FFF we would like to quote all of ELIZA.1 except the word "Correct." This can be done easily enough, by splitting ELIZA.1 into two parts and storing the second part under a special label. The frame would then look like this:

Question: What Irishman wrote the play from which 'My Fair Lady' was adapted?

Answer.1   It was *George Bernard Shaw.*
Eliza.1   Correct. "DOOLITTLE"

Answer.23   *Shaw/G.B.S.*
Eliza.23   Yes, but please give his correct full name.

Answer.4   *Loewe*
Eliza.4   Frederick Loewe wrote the music for 'My Fair Lady.' Alan Jay Lerner wrote the book for it. But "DRAMATIST"

Answer.5   *Lerner*
Eliza.5   Alan Jay Lerner wrote the 'book' for 'My Fair Lady.' Frederick Loewe wrote the music. But "DRAMATIST"

Answer.6   *Rex Harrison*
Eliza.6   Rex Harrison played the part of Professor

Henry Higgins in the Broadway production and later in the film version, but "DRAMA-TIST"

Answer.7   The author of *'Pygmalion'*
Eliza.7   "DRAMATIST"

Answer.8   What is *'My Fair Lady'* about?
Eliza.8   The theme of both 'My Fair Lady' and 'Pygmalion,' the play on which it was based, is derived from the Greek story of a sculptor who . . . (etc.)

Answer.9   I thought *'My Fair Lady'* was a *musical.*/I thought *'My Fair Lady'* was a *movie.*

Eliza.9   'My Fair Lady' was indeed a musical production (subsequently made into a motion picture), but the story was not original. Alan Jay Lerner adapted it from a play by a well-known Irishman famous for his biting wit, red beard, vegetarianism, and socialist views. Who was he?

Answer.1112   "DOUBTFUL"
Eliza.1112   "ELIZA.FF"

Eliza.F   Sorry, I missed your meaning. Please re-word your answer.

Eliza.FF	You may remember him as the author of 'Pygmalion,' 'Man and Superman,' and 'The Intelligent Woman's Guide to Socialism and Capitalism'—a sort of perennial enfant terrible of English letters in the first decades of this century.
Eliza.FFF	It was George Bernard Shaw. "DOOLITTLE"
Doolittle	Shaw's 'Pygmalion' used the idea of the Greek legend of the sculptor of that name . . .(etc.)
Dramatist	The musical was adapted from 'Pygmalion,' a play which was written by the same man who wrote 'Back to Methuselah' and 'Major Barbara,' namely_____(?)

Many things remain to be done.

There's that subordinate problem with ELIZA.23, which we put on the shelf back on page 90. It will be recalled that we asked, in response to Answer.23 ("Shaw"), that the student supply the full name . . .

What happens if he expresses doubt, or says he doesn't know? His reply would match DOUBTFUL, and he would be given the message labelled ELIZA.FF as provided in ELIZA.1112. But this would be inappropriate, because he is already aware of Shaw's identity—although he might not remember Shaw's full name.

Or what happens if he guesses wrong? ("Samuel M. Shaw") This would match ELIZA.23 all over again, and we certainly don't want that.

Both difficulties are solved by inserting special controls: one just ahead of ELIZA.1112 telling the computer, in effect, "If the student used Answer.23 before getting here, *ignore* ELIZA.1112 and jump to ELIZA.FFF." The other is planted just ahead of ELIZA.23, telling the computer, "If you've been here before, go to ELIZA.23A." ELIZA.23A will simply say "Wrong," and then quote ELIZA.FFF. In this way we can disclose the full name and get on with more important instruction.

Another problem is presented by the possibility of endlessly looping the student who persists in expressing doubt. This can be prevented by inserting another control at DOUBTFUL, bypassing ELIZA.1112 after it has been used one or two times.

The author needn't worry about the form of these controls as long as he expresses clearly for the benefit of the coder exactly what he wants to do. In actual practice the author will quickly feel the need to adopt some mutually acceptable conventions to define his wishes. Unless he really wants to get embroiled in the mechanics of the program, however, he will choose symbols, abbreviations, and commands which do *not* coincide with the "official" code. This is because true operational codes often have hidden peculiarities with which only the coder will be conversant. If the author does coder's work for him, some of these may be overlooked. It is quite enough for the author/instructor to concern himself with the maze of the instruction, without taking on this added responsibility.

In Figure 3, the George Bernard Shaw frame is reproduced as it might appear in the recommended worksheet. Note that it has been re-cast in the form suggested in Chapter 5, with author-devised codes to indicate which entries are scan specifications and which are intended for display.

Please note also that we have stripped away labels which, for the present at least, appear to be unnecessary, because nowhere are they referred to. (SHAW.A is needed because it will be referred to elsewhere in the program, being the start of a frame.) We can always put them back in, if needed.

The order of some of the student-answer/computer-response combinations has been changed so as to make them work more reliably. Perhaps you already noticed the need for this. For example, suppose the student had said, "I don't think it was George Bernard Shaw." The scan for ELIZA.1 (in the original arrangement on page 92) would have been satisfied, and the student would have been told "Correct . . . (etc.)!" So we put DOUBTFUL ahead of the scan for *George Bernard Shaw,* to filter out such a response before it can reach the latter.

The following rule for the ordering of scans is recommended:

Scan first for unwanted elements ─────────────┐

Scan next for wanted elements ─────────────┐ │

Scan next for missing elements ─────────── ─ ┐ │

Scan last for miscellaneous elements ───── ─ ─ ┐ │

The process works this way:

    "It certainly *wasn't* George Bernard Shaw." ─┘

    "It was *George Bernard Shaw.*" ────────────┘

    "It was a fellow named *Shaw.*" ──────────────┘

    "It was the one who wrote *'Pygmalion.'*" ───────────┘

when the scan specifications consist of the italicized words.

FIGURE 3

		DISPLAY TEXT AND SCAN SPECIFICATIONS		COMMANDS
Labels	Codes	Operands	Codes	Operands
SHAW. A	DS	What Irishman wrote the play from which "My Fair Lady" was adapted?		
SHAW. 1	WM			
	SS	"DOUBTFUL"	DOM	If you've been here before, but haven't been to SHAW. 2, quote ELIZA. FFF and then jump to WAGER. A.
			DOM	If you've been here twice before quote ELIZA. FFF and then jump to WAGER. A
(ex-Eliza. 1122)	DSM	"ELIZA. FF"	DOM	Jump to SHAW. 1
	SS DSM	George Bernard Shaw Correct. "DOOLITTLE"	DOM	Jump to WAGER. A
	SS DSM	G. B. S. Shaw Yes, but please give his correct full name.	DOM	If you've been here before quote ELIZA. 23A and then jump to WAGER. A. Otherwise jump to SHAW. 1
	SS DSM	Lowew Lowe Loew Low (or just L**w*) Frederick Loewe wrote the music for "My Fair Lady." Alan Jay Lerner wrote the 'book' for it, but "DRAMATIST"	DOM	Jump to SHAW. 1
	SS DSM	Lerner Alan Jay Lerner wrote the 'book' for the musical, and Frederick Loewe wrote the music. But "DRAMATIST"		ditto
	SS DSM	Rex Harrison Actor Rex Harrison played the part of Professor Henry Higgins in the Broadway production of "My Fair Lady," and later in the movie, but "DRAMATIST"		ditto
	SS DSM	Pygma* "DRAMATIST"		ditto
	SS	My Fair Lady ? The theme of both "My Fair Lady" and "Pygmalion" (the play on which it was based,) is derived from the Greek legend of the sculptor who... (etc.)		ditto
	SS DSM	Movie Musical Show Cinema Motion "My Fair Lady" was indeed a musical production (subsequently made into a movie) but the story was not original. Alan Jay Lerner adapted it from a play by a well-known Englishman famous for his biting wit, red beard, vegetarianism, socialist views, and concern with linguistics. Who was he?		ditto
			DOF	Check to see if you've been here before. If so, jump to ELIZA. FF
	FM	I don't understand. Please re-word your reply.	DOF	Jump to SHAW. 1
ELIZA. FF	FM	You may remember him as the author of "Pygmalion," "Man and Superman," "The Intelligent Woman's Guide to Socialism and Capitalism" - a sort of enfant terrible of English letters in the first decades of this century.	DOF	Check to see if you've been here before. If so, jump to ELIZA. FFF
ELIZA. FFF	FM	It was George Bernard Shaw. "DOOLITTLE"	DOF	Jump to WAGER. A
DOOLITTLE	DS	Shaw's "Pygmalion" was based on the idea of the Greek legend of the sculptor who... (etc.)		
DRAMATIST	DS	The musical was adapted from "Pygmalion," a play by the same man who wrote "Back to Methuselah," "Major Barbara," and "Androcles and the Lion," namely_____?		
ELIZA. 23A	DS	Wrong. "ELIZA. FFF"		
DOUBTFUL	SS	*n't know do not know *n't remember give up hint got me help no idea *est idea no * certain not * sure stuck unsure uncertain confused sea search (Note: this item would be stored somewhere in a central location and would serve for all frames)		
WAGER	DS	(Beginning of next frame)		

FIGURE 4

DISPLAY TEXT AND SCAN SPECIFICATIONS			COMMANDS	
Labels	Codes	Operands	Codes	Operands
SHAW. A	DS	What Irishman wrote the play from which "My Fair Lady" was adapted?		
SHAW. 1	WM			
	SS	"DOUBTFUL"	DOM	If you've been here before, but haven't been to SHAW. 2, quote ELIZA. FFF and then jump to WAGER. A.
			DOM	If you've been here twice before quote ELIZA. FFF and then jump to WAGER. A
				Add 1 to DOUBTSCORE
(ex-Eliza. 1122)	DSM	"ELIZA. FF"	DOM	Jump to SHAW. 1
	SS	George Bernard Shaw	DOM	Jump to WAGER. A
	DSM	Correct. "DOOLITTLE"		
	SS	G. B. S. Shaw	DOM	If you've been here before quote ELIZA. 23A and then jump to WAGER. A. Otherwise jump to SHAW. 1
	DSM	Yes, but please give his correct full name.		
	SS	Lowew Lowe Loew Low (or just L**w*)		
	DSM	Frederick Loewe wrote the music for "My Fair Lady." Alan Jay Lerner wrote the 'book' for it, but "DRAMATIST"	DOM	Jump to SHAW. 1
	SS	Lerner		
	DSM	Alan Jay Lerner wrote the 'book' for the musical, and Frederick Loewe wrote the music. But "DRAMATIST"		ditto
	SS	Rex Harrison		
	DSM	Actor Rex Harrison played the part of Professor Henry Higgins in the Broadway production of "My Fair Lady," and later in the movie, but "DRAMATIST"		ditto
	SS	Pygma*		
	DSM	"DRAMATIST"		ditto
	SS	My Fair Lady ?		Add 1 to SHAKY
		The theme of both "My Fair Lady" and "Pygmalion" (the play on which it was based,) is derived from the Greek legend of the sculptor who... (etc.)		ditto
	SS	Movie Musical Show Cinema Motion		
	DSM	"My Fair Lady" was indeed a musical production (subsequently made into a movie) but the story was not original. Alan Jay Lerner adapted it from a play by a well-know Englishman famous for his biting wit, red beard, vegetarianism, socialist views, and concern with linguistics. Who was he?		ditto
			DOF	Check to see if you've been here before. If so, jump to ELIZA. FF
	FM	I don't understand. Please re-word your reply.	DOF	Jump to SHAW. 1
ELIZA. FF	FM	You may remember him as the author of "Pygmalion," "Man and Superman," "The Intelligent Woman's Guide to Socialism and Capitalism" - a sort of enfant terrible of English letters in the first decades of this century.	DOF	Check to see if you've been here before. If so, jump to ELIZA. FFF
ELIZA. FFF	FM	It was George Bernard Shaw. "DOOLITTLE"	DOF	Jump to WAGER. A
DOOLITTLE	DS	Shaw's "Pygmalion" was based on the idea of the Greek legend of the sculptor who... (etc.)		
DRAMATIST	DS	The musical was adapted from "Pygmalion," a play by the same man who wrote "Back to Methuselah," "Major Barbara," and "Androcles and the Lion," namely_____?		Add 1 to SHAWSCORE,
ELIZA. 23A	DS	Wrong. "ELIZA. FFF"		
DOUBTFUL	SS	*n't know do not know *n't remember give up hint got me help no idea *est idea no * certain not * sure stuck unsure uncertain confused sea search (Note: this item would be stored somewhere in a central location and would serve for all frames)		
WAGER	DS	(Beginning of next frame)		

TEST DIALOGUES

I.   Instructor: What Irish playwright wrote
                                    the play from which MY
                                    FAIR LADY was adapted?

                      Student: I don't recall.

                      Instructor: You may remember him as the
                                    author of PYGMALION, MAN
                                    AND SUPERMAN, and THE
                                    INTELLIGENT WOMAN'S
                                    GUIDE TO SOCIALISM AND
                                    CAPITALISM—a sort of per-
                                    ennial enfant terrible of Eng-
                                    lish letters in the first decades
                                    of this century.

                      Student: Oh, I remember, it was Shaw.

                      Instructor: Yes, but please give his full
                                    name.

                      Student: It was—I'm not sure.

                      Instructor: It was George Bernard Shaw.
                                    Shaw's PYGMALION was

based on the Greek legend of
the sculptor who . . . (etc.)

Instructor: (next frame)

II. Instructor: What Irish playwright
. . . (etc.)

Student: Rex Harrison.

Instructor: Actor Rex Harrison played the
part of Professor Higgins in
the Broadway production of
MY FAIR LADY, and later in
the movie, but the musical was
adapted from a play by the
same man who wrote BACK
TO METHUSELAH, MAJOR
BARBARA, and ANDRO-
CLES AND THE LION, name-
ly_____?

Student: Was it Shaw?

Instructor: Yes, but please give his current
full name.

Student: Sir William Shaw.

Instructor: Wrong. It was George Bernard
                  Shaw. Shaw's PYGMALION
                  was based on the idea of the
                  Greek legend of the sculptor
                  who . . . (etc.)

Instructor: (next frame)

III.   Instructor: W h a t   I r i s h   playwright
                  . . . (etc.)

        Student: I saw the movie. Was it on
                  Broadway too?

        Instructor: MY FAIR LADY was indeed a
                  musical production (subse-
                  quently made into a movie)
                  but the story was not original.
                  Alan Jay Lerner adapted it
                  from a play by a well-known
                  Irishman famous for his biting
                  wit, red beard, vegetarianism,
                  socialist views, and concern
                  with linguistics. Who was he?

Student: Ibsen?

Instructor: You may remember him as the
                 author   of   PYGMALION
                 . . . (etc.)

Student: I'm sure I never heard of him.

Instructor: It was George Bernard Shaw.
                 Shaw's PYGMALION was
                 based on the idea of the Greek
                 legend of the sculptor who
                 . . . (etc.)

Instructor: (next frame)

IV.   Instructor: What Irish playwright wrote
                        the play . . . (etc.)

       Student: I didn't see MY FAIR LADY.

       Instructor: I don't understand. Please re-
                        word your reply.

       Student: What I mean is I haven't the
                        slightest idea who you're talk-
                        ing about.

Instructor: You may remember him as the author of PYGMALION, MAN AND SUPERMAN, and THE INTELLIGENT WOMAN'S GUIDE TO SOCIALISM AND CAPITALISM—a sort of enfant terrible of English letters in the first decades of this century.

Student: Oh, you mean Shaw—George Bernard Shaw.

Instructor: Correct. Shaw's PYGMALION was based on the idea of the Greek legend of the sculptor who . . . (etc.)

(Note how the *ordering* of the first two scans prevents the following contretemps:)

Student: Oh, you mean Shaw—George Bernard Shaw.

Instructor: Yes, but please give his correct full name.

Student: I just did!

Instructor: Wrong. It was George Bernard Shaw. Shaw's PYGMALION, etc.

Instructor: (next frame).

MORE MECHANISMS

10.

MORE MECHANISMS

There are ways of guarding against misinterpretation of a student's answer to a question, notably by asking him to confirm a particular meaning. This can be done *within* the frame under consideration, as an integral subroutine, or it can be accomplished externally.

ALICE.A/Question: What is the difference between a raven and a writing desk?

Alice.1   WM   (assume first-pass answer:) "One difference is the number of legs."

                (assume second-pass answer:) "Yes."

SS	legs
DSM	You mean a writing desk has more legs than a raven?
DOM	Jump to ALICE.1

SS	Writing desk more legs/YES
DSM	Correct. Anything else?

Note that the answer to the second subordinate question, if handled integrally, would result in erroneous looping. So a separate frame is required:

DOM	Jump to ALICE.B (or ALICE.2) (followed by additional SS/DSM/DOM combinations)

ALICE.B (DS blank)

ALICE.2	WM	_____
	SS	Yes
	DSM	Such as?
	DOM	Jump to ALICE.1
	SS	No
	DSM	Well, it seems to me that . . . (etc.)
	DOM	Jump to_____

External subroutines may not be as elegant as those which are integral with a main frame, but they are less vulnerable to ambiguities, and are easier both to construct and to repair.

A student's response may be quoted right back at him, if desired. This adds a note of realism to fail-match and other statements, such as:

"ALICE.1" is wrong.

I wasn't expecting you to say "ALICE.1." Please reconsider.

"ALICE.1?" No. Try re-wording your reply.

I don't understand what you mean by "ALICE.1." Please rephrase your answer.

I was hoping you'd say something other than "ALICE.1." A better answer would have been . . . (etc.)

There is danger here. Since any F answers (A_I, A_U, and A_{LPF}) will be quoted, the FM display resulting can be fairly inane. Try running an ALICE.1 of "I hate computers" through the above.

Student answers can also be stored for future reference, such as a consolidated listing for statistical purposes or for study leading to refinement of scan specifications. Or they can be quoted back to the student during a review sequence.

A wait-mode operation code (such as the "WM" we have been using) creates a space for a "text variable," and text created by the student is inserted in that space. Thereafter the contents may be moved around, analyzed, combined with other text variables, and so on, as long as they are accessible through some distinctive label. The author can accomplish these things by indicating to the coder something like "DO ADD ALICE.1 TO WONDERLIST."

One convenient use of the text variable is to store the student's name in a conversational form, and to use it occasionally during the running of the course. For instance if a student signs in as Miss Mary White at the beginning of the course, an initial DO command could provide for storage of either *Miss White* or *Mary* under a label such as NAME. This permits saying things like:

I should explain at this point, Miss White, that a raven-
. . . (etc.)

Another type of variable is used for storing numbers. These variables may be thought of as remote pigeon-holes whose contents may be added to, subtracted from, compared, replaced, or simply eradicated—at any time. All, of course, are referred to by label.

Numerical variables are used extensively as control devices to influence program decisions, such as by-passes, the calling-forth of subroutines, and many kinds of branching.

Their use for these purposes is in the coder's province and need not concern the author/instructor as long as the latter is aware that anything that can be counted may be so utilized.

The author/instructor should, however, participate in planning the range of numerical variables to be used in scoring. Almost anything he wants to keep track of can be recorded. For example one set of tallies could record a student's performance on certain types of questions. Another set could record his performance in various segments of the course. Another set could record the percentage of student response falling through to fail-match. Still another set could record speed of response. Naturally the computer's ability to keep track of all these things (almost) simultaneously makes it a powerful tool for educational research. But it also serves the immediate purposes of the author/instructor very well too.

It is recommended that the author/instructor list in advance as many different scoring tallies as he expects he will need. It would also be a good idea for him to note them in the margin of a copy of his syllabus, opposite the items to which they will apply.

Before affixing scoring weights to individual SS/DSM combinations in a frame, the author/instructor should look at the frame as a whole and decide just how much it should be weighted, as a whole, for worst-case performance. For example, he might decide that no matter how badly a student might do on the "My Fair Lady" frame, he would assign a negative score of no more than 3 for the whole performance.

This limit should be clearly noted at the end of the frame, so that the coder will be sure to provide for reduction of actual scores exceeding this figure. The author/instructor then assigns individual scores to specific SS/DSM and FM items. Figure 4 shows how he might annotate the worksheet for this purpose.

Although the student may assume that his progress is being recorded, there is no point in advertising to him the range and intricacy of the process. This would be almost as unnerving for him as a session with a human tutor in which the latter took copious notes, used a tape recorder and kept clattering away at an adding machine during the interview.

It is not necessary that scoring mechanisms be implemented when the program is first put on line for testing, except insofar as they may be needed for program decision purposes. In fact, it is probably better to wait until the first round of debugging and revision has been accomplished before adding anything not directly required for the running of the program.

There are many useful devices which one can insert at convenience, after the program has been compiled and tested in its main features. An example which comes to mind is an extra scan in each frame by means of which a student can ask for (and get) a display of the preceding question. This could be specified, encoded, keypunched and inserted in the "source" program any time the author and coder get around to it. The ease of making minor additions and changes cleanly is one of the attractive features of working with a computer.

CONCLUSION

11.

CONCLUSION

I remember one time assembling a hi-fi set from a jumble of wires, resistors, condensers, tubes, nuts, screws and other oddments supplied by a kit manufacturer. After engrossing many evenings and splattering much hot solder around the kitchen, I finally managed to get the thing put together, the front panel in place, the shiny knobs on their spindles. I plugged it into a wall socket. The tubes lit up. Then . . . a human voice! Music! It worked!

The elation surrounding that event best describes the elation felt the first time one sits down before a computer terminal and talks to one's own program. It may not work very well the first time (the hi-fi set didn't either) but the amazing thing is that it works at all.

Even though the author/instructor going through the

program is really talking to himself, the exchange takes on a remarkable freshness and clarity. In his role as a student he asserts a single, unique answer to each of the questions for which many different answers had been contemplated. He is momentarily free of impedimenta. He can observe the true rhythm of the dialogue—here perhaps too heavy and verbose, there a little too fragmentary and jumpy.

All the "right" replies of the student are soon checked out. The author/instructor will be more interested in seeing how the mavericks are dealt with, and as soon as his own imagination flags he will enlist that of bystanders. One should be prepared for spotty results, but sometimes a bit of logic comes through beautifully in spite of all the twists and turns of a perverse student. These first live encounters are always full of surprises.

Instead of berating himself for overlooking a perfectly natural response called up by one of his questions, the author (by now well versed in coping one by one with key elements) will be impatient to make the necessary change and get it into the machine. Some systems have an on-line "author mode" which permits dynamic editing of text. More commonly one must wait until enough changes have been written, keypunched and inserted into the source deck to make it worthwhile to recompile the entire program in the computer—a fairly expensive operation.

Much of the initial revision will be mechanistic: the removal of simple "bugs" which no coder or keypuncher can utterly exclude from a sizeable new program . . . loose ends, misplaced delimiters, transposed cards in the source deck, and so on. Concurrently the author and the coder will work together to improve scan specifications all along the line in order to prevent valid keywords from slipping through to fail-match. This, too, is a somewhat mechanistic function.

As such problems recede, the kind of work I call "pedagogical debugging" begins. And here it is that this Introduction and Guide must draw to a close, because each author/instructor will carry out pedagogical debugging in his own way—testing, observing, calling for opinions, adding new frames, scrapping old ones, and providing additional pathways through his material.

In this phase the author/instructor reaps the rewards of foresight, for careful planning, for early definition of goals and for conscientious formulation of syllabus and text. It is not a time to be unduly prolonged in a vain effort to please everybody. The teacher needs to decide at last when to say "That's it!" and to walk away.

I think such a point is reached when the system operates to the satisfaction of the real users—the students. They are, in the last analysis, the ones who know best if the system works for them. Do they take pleasure in terminal sessions? Do they feel that the unseen instructor really understands them most of the time? Do their subsequent inquiries show stimulus? These are the questions to ask in trying to arrive at some kind of evaluation.

The educator who undertakes to write a course of instruction for CAI will oftentimes wonder if the investment of time and effort is really worthwhile in terms of net results. For this there is no clear-cut answer. Currently, a great deal of research is going forward to streamline the total process of creating and implementing various types of CAI. In some development projects the thrust is toward achieving the lowest possible cost per student hour of on-line instruction, aiming, indeed, at net economies over traditional classroom methods. In others the thrust is toward development of programs which—although they may initially cost more than conventional lecture mode—will be at least as effective, yet much faster and more adaptive to individual learning needs. In view of today's increasing demands on the educational system and on the time of teachers and students alike, perhaps the latter objective carries the greater urgency.

How far we may go, and to what extent the new medium may prove useful throughout the educational spectrum, will be sensed only after a great many people have tried their hand with it. The knowledge and experience thus gained should in the long run prove worthwhile, both to the individual worker and to society.

APPENDIX

APPENDIX

Brudner, Harvey J. *Computer-based instruction.* Science. 162:3856 (Nov. 1968) pp. 46-50.

Dick, Walter *The development and current status of computer based instruction.* American Educational Research Journal. 2:1 (Jan. 1965) pp. 41-53.

Feurzig, Wallace *New instructional potentials of information technology.* IEEE Transactions on Human Factors in Electronics. HFE-8:2 (June 1967) pp. 84-88.

Frye, Charles H. *CAI languages; capabilities and applications.* Datamation. 14:9 (Sept. 1968) pp. 34-37.

Gordon, Robert M. *Computer-based instruction: some operational aspects.* Datamation. 15:1 (Jan. 1969) pp. 37-44.

Hanson, Duncan *Computer-assisted instruction and the individualization process.* In Annual Progress Report, Jan. 1, 1968 through Dec. 31, 1968, of the CAI Center, Institute of Human Learning, Florida State University. Rep. No. 7, (Jan. 1, 1969) pp. 139-152.

Hughes, Arthur D. *Desired characteristics of automated display consoles.* Proceedings of the Society for Information Display, 1:1 (Winter 1969) pp. 46-50.

Interuniversity Communications Council. *Future of the computer tutor.* In EDUCOM Bulletin (Hilda Jones, ed.) 2:4 (Sept. 1967) pp. 5-8.

do. *A CAI sampler: other examples.* Ibid. pp. 10-11.

Kurland, Norman D. *The impact of technology on education.* Educational Technology. 8:20 (Oct. 30, 1968) pp. 12-15.

Lekan, Helen, ed. *Index to computer assisted instruction.* Milwaukee, Wisc., Instructional Media Laboratory, University of Wisconsin.

Margolin, Joseph *The computer in education: Whose mission? What problem? Who adapts to whose needs?* Educational Technology. 8:24 (Dec. 30, 1968) pp. 9-12.

Markle, S.M. *Good frames and bad; a grammar of frame writing.* Wiley, New York (1964).

Maron, M.E., Humphrey, A.J. & Meredith, J.C. *An Information Processing Laboratory for Education and Research in Library Science: Phase I Final Report.* Institute of Library Research, University of California (July 1969).

McLendon, Paul *Teaching Teachers to Develop Software: an EDTECH Project.* AEDS Monitor. 7:8(March 1969) pp. 6-8.

Rath, Gustave J. *The development of computer-assisted instruction.* (R) IEEE Transactions on Human Factors in Electronics. HFE-8 (June 1967) pp. 60-63.

Reynolds, Donald *CAI within a systems approach to instruction.* AEDS Convention, Fort Worth, Texas, May 3, 1968. (14pp.)

Rogers, James L. *Current problems in CAI.* Datamation. 14:9 (Sept. 1968) pp. 28-33.

Saunders, Robert M. *Computer assisted learning: a progress report.* Engineering Education. (April 1968) pp. 927-930.

Silberman, H.F. & Filep, R.T. *Information systems applications in education.* Annual Review of Information Science. 3:2, pp. 357-395.

Silvern, Gloria M. & Leonard C. *Computer-assisted instruction: specifications for CAI programs and programmers.* Proceedings of the 21st Annual Conference of the Association for Computing Machinery. ACM Publ. P-66. (Thompson Book Co., Washington, D.C., 1966) pp. 57-65.

Stolurow, L.M. (1) *What is computer-assisted instruction?* (editorial) Educational Technology. (Aug. 15,1968) pp. 10-11.

do. (2) *Some factors in the design of systems for computer-assisted instruction.* Harvard Computing Technical Report No.7. Harvard University. May 1, 1968. (43pp.)

Uhr, Leonard *The compilation of natural language text into teaching machine programs.* Proceedings of the Fall Joint Computer Conference, 1964. Vol. 26, pp. 35-44.

do. *Toward the compilation of books into teaching machines.* IEEE Transactions on Human Factors in Electronics. HFE-8 (June 1967) pp. 81-84.

Ullmer, Eldon J. *The meaning of instructional technology: an operational analysis.* Educational Technology. 8:23 (Dec. 15, 1968) pp. 10-14.

Zinn, Karl L. *Programming conversational use of computers for instruction.* Proceedings of the 23rd National Conference of the Association for Computing Machinery. ACM Publ. P-68 (Aug. 1968) pp. 85-92.